Hey There Soc

How to Become a Social Freak and a Social Data Genius and Guru

By: Margaret Sanders

9781680322385

PUBLISHERS NOTES

Disclaimer – Speedy Publishing LLC

Speedy Publishing LLC

40 E Main Street, Newark, Delaware, 19711

Contact Us: 1-888-248-4521

Website: http://www.speedypublishing.co

REPRINTED Paperback Edition: ISBN: 9781680322385

Manufactured in the United States of America

DEDICATION

I dedicate this book to everyone who has low self-confidence and oftentimes being picked on. This book is a perfect guide for you on how to standout in the society.

TABLE OF CONTENTS

CHAPTER 1- CLIMB YOUR WAY UP TO SOCIAL LADDER

Taking time to discover what talent you have would help a lot in enhancing the way you feel regarding yourself. Besides, it lets you love and appreciate yourself more. Every person has his or her own talent – it's a special gift given by God.

So when someone asks you about your talent, what is your answer to him or her? If you don't know what's your talent yet then it's the right time for you to make a move and to find the right response to that question.

There are some things you can do to determine your hidden talent. Why don't you explore the history of your family and find out the talents possessed by your sisters or brothers or your father or mother? Are there singers, artists or dancers in your ancestry?

Hey There Socialite!

Typically, a child inherits not only the appearance of his or her father or mother but he or she can also inherit the talent that either his or her father or mother has. It's because talents have a tendency to run in a family and knowing your inherited talent can spark a brand new path to your life.

Then, try to recall those things you like the most or to where you are good at when you were just a kid. This particular stage of life is where a person is exposed to various activities or any class subjects that require a particular skill or talent. If you have put them out of your way for such a long period of time, today could be the right time for you to bring back to life your childhood talent.

Then now, you should think about the present. Think of something that is very interesting to you today. It can be a small spark of a thought. It might not be too huge at first yet it's something that you can feel deep within your soul. Or, it can be just something you are good at. You may get a piece of piece and write down all ideas that you may desire to pursue. Focus on those things you really like.

As soon as you have found your talent, you should pursue that with dedication, determination and full willingness to show what you've got to the entire world. Pursue that talent with all your heart. Your talent will take you to where you can be because it will help you develop more confidence.

Your talent will change the way you value yourself. Knowing your talent lets you build higher self-esteem. So, take some time today to rediscover who you are, use your talent and be proud to show others what you can do. All your efforts will be paid and you will be few steps away from what will make you proud of yourself.

Be active in Any School Activities

As a student, you will encounter certain situations wherein your teacher will encourage you to join in group events. Why don't you follow your teacher if you know that will bring good to you? Are you a kind of student who is very shy but is willing to overcome such character? If you answered "yes" to this question then you should try to interact with other students through joining the group events you like.

It's not only an opportunity to meet new people and make friends with them but it can also be the right timing to learn and develop some things that will make you a better student.

Did you know that group events can empower you to make your own decisions? Aside from that, it can help you earn vital experience and some sorts of skills that will lead you to the right path going to your future.

With your willingness to join in group events, you will be able to show your good traits. For instance, if you have the heart to help someone, you can take these events as opportunities to practice such trait.

Being active when it comes to group activities lets you embrace diversity and gain motivation. Besides, it is a way for you to learn how to work with other people effectively.

If you are one of those people who find a hard time to develop some skills then you should consider the importance of participating in the group events.

You can develop your communication and problem solving skills by joining any group activities that are held within the school. Being an active participant of group events also gives you the chance to become more engaged in campus life which you will really enjoy.

These activities will also let you learn the available resources within your school and you will be given the freedom to use them. If you have the interest to act as a leader then being an active group event participant will help you evaluate and improve your leadership way. It also builds a professional and academic network.

Types of Student Group Events You Should Consider

There can be numerous activities held throughout a school year. If you want to gain the benefits mentioned previously then you should start thinking of joining to any of these group events:

• Performing arts

• Publications

• Student organizations

• Departmental

• Athletic activities

• Group contests such as quiz bees

There can be other group events that your school permits and supports. Just pick those events you like the most or those activities where you can find those students who have the same interests with you if you will be more at ease if they are your companions. So what are you waiting for? Have fun with your life as a student by exposing yourself to group events.

Chapter 2- Bring Out that Leadership Skill in You and be Socially Recognized

Every person can develop his or her leadership skills through volunteering. If you have the desire to become a leader, you need to develop some skills that should be manifested by an efficient leader.

Volunteerism enhances and develops these skills including other important skills like problem solving, mentoring, communicating and coaching effectively.

Your leadership skills will be developed only when you do your part. The following are certain ways on how you can improve most leadership skills by means of volunteering:

Develop People's Skills

Your interpersonal skills will be developed when you prefer to work along with other people from various backgrounds. Through volunteering, a person will learn the best way to handle different people and diverse situations. With your willingness to be a volunteer, you'll learn the significance of strong communication, diversity, mutual respect, cooperation, shared planning and exerting effort to meet common goals.

Develop Your Confidence

Volunteering gives opportunities to face new challenges with no fear of career or financial repercussions. Learning and developing new skills within a low-consequence and supportive environment will assist you in expanding your skills and in gaining confidence.

Learn Organization or Planning Skills

A volunteer learns to plan efficient meetings, organize parties or events and direct other volunteers. Through event planning, you will learn the best and proper way to set your goals, delineate actions and track the results. These planning & organization abilities are moveable through the entire career directions.

Improve Mentoring Skills

Most volunteer groups depend on other volunteers to distribute knowledge and information. As you get a new role inside an organization, you're often encouraged to guide the new member assuming your previous role.

Enhance Communication Skills

Leadership needs clear, organized and concise communications. Volunteer activities usually require a person to communicate what he or she does and to sway others to support your cause.

Develop Time Management Skills

Volunteering demands the need to learn the right way to organize your work, family & volunteer priorities. To keep a sensible balance, you have to learn how you should manage time.

If you have all of these skills, it will not be hard for you to learn how you should act to become an efficient leader. Everything starts by your willingness to work as a volunteer so make a move today and be a good leader someday.

Man with Honor

One law of social makeup is that a person must be reliable. It only means that you should do what you promised to do. If you are reliable, others will surely put their trust in you. People are not willing to deal with unreliable individuals but they always look for someone who is "a man of his word". If you are a kind of person who knows the value of becoming a reliable, you understand how it feels to know that you are okay to others.

The Advantages of Being a Reliable Person

Certainly, you want to deal with someone you can really count on. Inside a school, a teacher admires those students who practice reliability and those who always come to school on a timely manner and complete their homework and projects on or before the deadlines.

The main benefit of being a trustworthy is that people around you feel that you are the person they can rely on at all times. A reliable individual will be able to make new friends easily than someone who's not careful when it comes to personal relationships & cannot be counted on to keep his or her word.

A student who is reliable is often asked by a teacher to handle a certain task and he or she is expected to complete that on time. He or she will reap rewards of praises and recognition right after he or she reported that the task is already completed. That student will feel happy and good because of that.

If you are reliable, most people will admire you. This is primarily because reliability is a very admirable trait. Everybody dislikes dealing with those people who are not committed and true to what they say so being dependable is a trait you should develop as a student.

If you are reliable, you'll get good reputation and you will be able to avoid dispute with someone which unreliable individuals often experience. You will experience a very wonderful feeling as you choose to be "a man or woman of his or her word".

So how will you be able to develop this trait? If you don't know what's the best thing to do then you must follow these steps:

Steps to Follow on How to Become a "Man of Your Word"

Make a plan. Ensure that you will start taking the easiest steps if you really want to keep your word.

Be true to what you say that you'll do. If you make promises, work with all your heart to do them for real. Always keep in your mind that you won't be successful in life if you will not be able to do what you promised to someone or even to yourself.

Keep a reminder. You have your latest model of phone that you can use to remind yourself about your plan. Why don't you set a reminder in your precious phone? It will help you a lot.

Provide yourself with time. If you need to go somewhere else, you should think of how long you have to travel so that you can get there. Make sure that all those things you need are already prepared. You must be apt in your time objectives.

Avoid making excuses and don't lie. If you find a hard time in keeping your word, don't make excuses or pretend that you were able to make it though you failed actually.

Learn to refuse. When you have some plans already, you should make more plans but focus on your existing ones.

If you failed, don't forget to apologize. Regardless of your reason why you failed to keep your word, still, you should apologize. It is okay if it happens as long as you know that you did everything just to be "a man or woman of your word".

CHAPTER 3- GET UP AND BE SOCIALLY ACCEPTED

A student like you can learn how to establish friendships and relate socially with children and adults while you are at the school. Unfortunately, social expectations and friendships usually trigger stress to teenagers especially to a student who faces social problems. Typical social problems that often take place inside the schools are peer pressure, cliques and bullying.

Peer Pressure

This happens when a student affects the decisions of another student. Peer pressure could be positive and an example of this is when you tell again your friend regarding the homework or when you push her to join in any sports team. On the other hand, peer pressure can be negative such as the pressure to consume alcohol, cut classes, smoke cigarettes, cheat on the exam and do some sorts of crimes like shoplifting. Students like you typically find it hard and stressful to resist peer pressure.

Bullying

Bullying happens when a student is frequently picked on by another student who is more influential than he or she is. A student who looks unusual or from a different religion and race, or may be a lesbian or gay is typically a victim of bullying.

This negative thing could be physical like tripping and hitting or verbal like teasing and taunting. A student, whether that person is a girl or a boy, can become a bully or the bullying victim.

Cliques

Cliques pertain to a group of students that reject other students. Cliques typically come with codes of attitude like the need to dress in a particular way or to play and have fun with a specific sport.

Cliques typically insult or bully the outsiders and if you will be a member of a clique, you may find it harmful and stressful since cliques generally discourage the members from hanging out with someone else. The members of the group are also required to act in a certain way just to fit in.

Getting Help

If you are struggling with any social problems inside the school, you should not feel that you are the only person who experiences such type of situation. You can talk to your parents or to your teacher if you are in physical threat because of bullying or if you've made wrong choices due to peer pressure.

Always keep in your mind that everything will be fine and what is happening to you right now is just a challenge of life. You should not be afraid to build friendships with those who are not like you. Spend more time with your most trusted friends and participate in the activities that will really make you happy.

Learn From Your Mistakes and Move On

Nobody wants to make mistakes as most people view the act of making these as a failure. People are afraid of failure so they always try their very best not to make mistakes. They feel so bad when they were able to do something wrong. If you are one of those people who have this kind of viewpoint when it comes to making mistakes, you should open your eyes and look at the brighter side of the problem.

If you make mistakes, it does not mean that you need to punish yourself. You should not be afraid of making mistakes because you can get lessons from these. It means that your faults will teach you what to do next time to avoid failure.

The usual thing that happens when someone made mistakes is that he or she tries to justify his or her actions to conceal his or her faults. This attitude is not good, don't you know that? With this behavior, you will not be able to learn from your mistakes. If you will not learn and understand the lessons behind your blunders, you will never improve.

The most crucial aspect of making mistakes is to admit them. If the situation affects only you, ensure that you really know what you have done and document that. But, if the scenario is affecting people around you, confess your mistakes and think of those things that you can supposedly do to avoid them. You must also document them as well.

To make sure that you will learn from your mistakes, you should keep in mind the following tips:

You need to identify your mistakes. If they are obvious then it will not be hard for you to do the job. When you don't know the reason why something bad happened, you can seek help from other people and get their standpoint. Once the problem has been identified, don't forget to document it and think of some actions to be taken to prevent the problem from happening once again.

Admit your mistakes. After identifying your mistakes, you should admit them. Accept the fact that you have made them because if you deny them, you will not learn how to get up and make a change for your own good. Remember that mistakes have lessons that you should bear in mind to avoid making the same things again and again.

Make a list of your mistakes and include the actions to be taken so that you can prevent the reoccurrence of those faults you have done before. Label the journal where you listed these things as "mistakes". Keep the journal readily available for frequent reviewing. When you review your faults, you would find the actions you've taken that will be helpful in any problem that you might be encountering.

Implement the new things you have learned. As said before, your mistakes are trying to teach you certain lessons which you should apply into your everyday living. Apply what you've learned from recognizing, accepting and documenting your faults.

Hey There Socialite!

If you will look at your mistakes positively and you follow these suggestions, you have a higher chance to obtain a continuous improvement. So while you are still a student, you should break your habit of denying your faults. Start your struggle to learn from your mistakes today!

Make it Your Call

A student needs to be responsible in every step of the way. You should keep in mind that you need to take up responsibilities in your assignments. You need to complete them on time and you should comply with the rules.

Oftentimes, students are asked by their teachers to group themselves and each group may consist of five or more members. Every group will have its own homework.

Of course, a group will have a leader who will be responsible for making sure that every step will be taken to ensure the project's success.

But, the success of the whole project does not rely only on the leader but it depends on each member of the group. Thus, every member should be responsible enough and be determined to work together to meet success.

Every member must work hand in hand with his or her colleagues. Coordination and cooperation are very important in this situation.

In a group activity, each member is often assigned to handle a particular segment of the project. It means that every member will be obliged to complete a certain segment of the group homework. So, whatever job is assigned to you, be sure that you will be responsible for that. You must take responsibility in your assignment.

Spend time and pay adequate attention to it. Be determined to fulfill your duty as a member of the group. Show to your group members that you are dependable and responsible. Be patient and always keep in your mind that your efforts will be paid in the end.

If you will not take up responsibilities in your assignment, the negative effect on it will greatly affect not only you but the whole group. As all of the members of the group are doing their part except you, their efforts will just be wasted because you failed to do yours. They will blame you for your negligence especially if the result of the project will not be good though they tried to solve the problem. You don't want it to happen, isn't it?

So, you must be responsible right from the start. If you can do the job today, why would you prefer to do it tomorrow? If this is your usual habit today, make a change and be ready to face your responsibility to complete your assignment.

CHAPTER 4- RESPECT OTHERS AND BE MORE SOCIABLE

Meeting new people and making them friends is one of the most important things that you should do in life. If you enter a new school, one of the things you will have to do is to make your classmates as your new friends.

Do you wish to have more friends but you don't know what to do? Don't worry! With a little technique and a positive viewpoint, you will be able to make your own circle of friends in just a very short period of time.

The first thing you should do is to go out to meet other students. Before you can make new friends, you need to meet different people. If you are new to a community, you can branch out from simply meeting your classmates.

Why don't you check the local bulletin board to know the activities that will be held within your community? You can attend at least one of those events and begin talking to others.

You also need to be friendly. When you meet new people, you should not forget that you have to smile, keep eye contact and offer your hand for a shake.

You should bear extra confidence and keep in mind that overly introverted attitude could appear across as standoffish or snobbish.

Find usual interests. You can mention some of your interests and hobbies to find out those people who share the same interest with you. If you find somebody who does, keep your attention to him or her. On the other hand, when no one shares the same interest with you, move forward. You must not be discouraged but keep on trying. Don't lose hope.

Also, you need to listen to what other people say. You must pay adequate attention to those people you are meeting. Look at them one by one as your potential new friend with a particular interest.

Do not forget to find out their interest while you talk to them. Show appreciation when other people show true care regarding shared interests and concerns.

Hold a simple and small party. You can organize a get-together at your residence. You can make it either a large or a simple and small party; just choose what suits you.

Prepare some recipes and drinks and few games or movies to avoid any awkward interlude.

Hey There Socialite!

You should wait for someone to invite you to go out and have fun. If you are the only one who initiates contact, it's your turn to wait for your new friends to ask you to go with them.

It will give you the chance to meet the inner circle of your friends. Hopefully, some of them may become your new friends too. Rest assured that you will find yourself having a big circle of friends someday.

Every person is unique and you will notice that each and every person around you differs significantly from you. This can turn into a challenge to respect individual differences for it is really hard to understand someone else who is very different from you.

One of the problems that you may encounter in this kind of situation is that you face difficulties in finding the best way to treat the person. This is primarily because you do not have any experience with the way of living of that person. You don't know what his or her beliefs in life are.

On the other hand, it is very important for you to learn how to understand the differences between you and your friend, teacher or anyone you meet every day inside the school. This way, you will be able to maintain harmony in your relationship with that person.

Instead of criticizing those differences, you should try to accept and embrace them. Whether you agree with his or her beliefs in life or not, still, that person deserves to gain respect. You must use this experience of yours as an instrument to learn & grow as an individual.

The road for this scenario will be full of obstacles but don't worry. You should not be afraid to take the challenge. All you just need to do is to follow these tips and rest assured that you will be on the right track:

-Learn more about your culture. Understanding your culture would help you a lot in understanding the effect of cultural behaviors and beliefs.

To learn how to respect individual differences, you must get to know someone from another culture as a person, first. When you deal with a person who is dissimilar from you, try to learn first more about him or her so that you can see and tell what makes him or her not the same with you.

It is very important to spend some of your time in talking to him or her. If you are dealing with a small group of persons within a formal situation, you can run a questionnaire so that you can obtain and collect information regarding these people. In that way, it will not be hard for you to determine how those people vary from you & from other members of the group.

- Then, you should proceed on trying to learn and understand other's culture. It is believed that respect starts by acknowledging the dignity, rights and opinions of each and every one.

You can start getting to know people around you by simply asking them some decent questions concerning their traditions and customs. When these people who came from another culture celebrate a special event or holiday, you may consider participating or urging them to share some pieces of information about that particular celebration.

This way, you will be more able to understand their culture and their differences from you.

Hey There Socialite!

- Learn to admit those things which are against your belief. Showing respect to the differences of a person from you does not mean that you will always say "yes" and agree with them. If there is a variance of opinion which cannot be overcome, you should move past it. Look at it as just a divergence of standpoints and not a subject of good and wrong.

- Share some details regarding your life. As the person or the group of people shared information about their culture and beliefs, you must reciprocate in detail-sharing by simply volunteering and giving information concerning your life. In that way, you can let the person see that you're willing and determined to build a relationship with him or her.

- Make connections where the similarities appear. You should look for those things that both you and the person with whom you have differences possess.

You should try to build on those similarities; come with him or her for a social gathering or you may start discussing some things the two of you enjoy. While you do these things, you would probably see that you and that person are actually more similar than you thought before.

If you will follow all of these tips, you will surely experience how easy it is to understand the differences between you and a certain person. So start doing what you can do today and be happy with the result.

Be Committed, Tough and Responsible

Do you wish to show off your resourcefulness? Well, you can do that in the best way by sharing what's on your mind. Yes, the key here is to share your knowledge.

Maybe you are wondering why you must share your knowledge to others especially to your classmates. If you are thinking of it as a wrongful action then you are definitely wrong. Actually, it's not only your classmates or someone else will benefit if you will be willing to share what you know but it will also bring good to you. Just consider the following benefits:

- If you will be eager to share your knowledge, your friends or your classmates will see you as an expert. They see you as someone who is resourceful, and clever.

- By sharing your information, people will start to admire you. They will become very interested to know more about you and they will think that you can help them a lot if they need someone who is resourceful like you.

- By sharing your ideas, those people around you especially your classmates will start to show their interest to spend more time with you. They will become your new friends in the long run not only because of your willingness to share your knowledge but for the reason that they simply admire your resourcefulness.

- You will be able to develop and enhance your skills in writing. As a part of sharing what you know, you will be asked to write down everything in detailed way. This will help in developing your skills in writing.

- You become a better speaker. Sharing your knowledge is also one of the ways to improve your communication skills. If you find a hard time in communicating with other people and you are afraid of standing and talking in front of others, knowledge sharing can help you in dealing with your problem.

If you become popular as an expert and you start sharing your ideas, it can lead you to opportunities to speak about your topic. You know more about the subject and it will let you focus your attention on the mechanics of speaking in the public.

Sharing your knowledge is a good way to develop some of your skills and it can lead you to great opportunities especially when you are already a working professional.

If you have creative ideas within your mind and you know a lot of things you think your friends or colleagues don't know yet, consider sharing those things and be surprised to the great possibilities that will come along your way.

CHAPTER 5- INCREASE SOCIAL INTERACTION THROUGH SOCIAL MEDIA

Busy people, with equally demanding and busy schedules today, almost always is the contributing factor for the lack of social interaction with others due to the lack of time. Therefore there is sometime the need for intervention and this can come in the package of social networking dating.

There are usually no physical boundaries, when it comes to meeting someone over the internet. Because the internet connection are so wide and popularly used it is possible to make a connection with someone as close as down the street or as far away as across the world.

Therefore when it comes to internet dating, social networking sites can and usually do feature member from all over the world and while also providing the localized list for those not so adventurous.

For those who are pressed for time and really don't want to go through the "vetting" stage that would involve the patience of physically having to meet and spend time with a person, this social networking dating option presents a very viable and effective platform.

Often the hassle of going on dates can not only be exhausting but also incur a lot of unnecessary cost of which the individual may not have the capacity to cope with.

Social networking sites for dating are also a good way to build up an individual's confidence levels and there is no real need for physical contact until both parties are ready to initiate the actual contact.

This is usually done only after both parties are ready and willing to take the next step. This is an ideal way to limit the possibility of enduring disappointments and ridicule.

Thinking of Online Dating?

There are several very glaring differences in these two seemingly similar platforms; however the distinctions mainly lie in the use and purpose of these sites.

For now both the social networking sites and the online dating sites present a very viable option to those using these platforms to further their own personal agenda.

Examples of social networking sites would include sites such as MySpace, Twitter and Facebook and these ideally provide the individual with access to other people's postings with the idea of keeping abreast with what in going on in their lives.

Opinions and events are often posted and most people find this sort of connections very fulfilling, enjoyable and interesting. The ability to chat, exchange information, seek opinions and generally just stay connected to a vast amount of people is why most people opt for the social networking sites.

There is no real underlying reason for this connection, and if a romantic liaison is formed then it is considered an added benefit and usually not the original of pressing intention of those participating in the social networking platform.

This is where the similarities start to differ between the sites, as most online dating sites consists of member who are serious in their intentions for signing up at such sites.

These intentions would include the actual exercise of going through the motions of finding and building a relationship with another party, with the eventual intention of making a permanent commitment.

The online dating sites generally provides the avenue for the individual to narrow down the search to a select few and then take the next step to initiate a connection.

The element of privacy is also much more of a consideration when it comes to online dating sites and not a lot of personal information is divulged or featured until connections are made and all parties concerned are ready and willing to divulge more information.

CHAPTER 6- LOVE IN SOCIAL MEDIA?

There are several stipulations that would generally be followed to ensure the dating exercise on the twitter platform stays pleasant and none threatening in any way or form.

Though, this is a comparatively fairly new inclusion into the dating avenue, twitter is fast making an impressive option to explore when it comes to online dating possibilities.

The following are some of the features that should be considered when making the decision to explore this particular style of social networking for the purpose of dating:

Twitter

The concept of providing lave matcher in less than 140 characters is something that most time restricted individual would be pleased to engage in. this short and often to the point style of communication and alerts is a welcomed introduction.

The information placed on the profiles will be sent to the Twitter followers, and those interested can then take the next step themselves and initiate contact.

If there is a private conversation that is designed and intended to stay that way, then the use of direct messaging is encouraged. This is necessary as it would be remembered that all communication done on twitter is privy to everyone else.

Thus by using direct messaging the communication is kept private until it is deemed fit to share it with the world.

Building the individual social networking exercise slowly, is also another important feature to remember, as too much activity at the site will then be interpreted as spam and will eventually cause a lot of problems for the users. This sudden influx of Twitter numbers is not advisable and should be avoided at all costs.

To avoid any future possible complications, it would be advisable to first start with making connections on Twitter within a certain radius and not simply go world wide as the sheer demographics can present a challenge to those intending to take the connection to the next level.

Although facebook was initially the ideal way to reconnect with people, friends and family, it is now becoming a compatible way to getting dates online.

Although caution should be exercised as many people would not really respond well to "cold" and "in your face" contact, therefore using the appropriate tools and profile introductions will help to demonstrate the individual's intentions without too much misconceptions and misinterpretations.

The following are some steps that are recommended, should an individual decide to explore the dating options using the facebook platform:

Facebook

Using the search bar provided scroll through the information feature based on the location and interests, then choose the profile that most interests the individual. When this is narrowed down to a few ideal choices, then click on the name or photo to preview the complete profile content.

Using the common interest as the main element for the connection would give the connection a better chance of achieving some success as the other party would be keener to be linked to like minded people.

In the send message prompt, type a simple and casual note explaining the interest in the party's profile content without being too overwhelming and "corny".

Initiate and engage in light conversation styles to ensure the other party responds. Remembering to keep everything light and friendly will help to create the comfortable aura that will encourage a response.

After the initial exchange of about 10 messages, adding the new contact to the friends list. Then the next possible step would be to invite the online new friend to a social activity that is publically located, and ensure the circumstances for the meeting are kept casual and light.

However, the initiator should be prepared for the response given, if it is unfavorable at the time, and perhaps make a similar invitation sometime later.

Facebook is fast becoming a popular way of informing anyone and everyone of an up and coming event that is being hosted or organized. Because of this very unique way of making invitations available to all, it is also a great way to meet new people or find dates.

The following are just some of the possibilities when it comes to finding dates at social events featured on facebook:

Facebook Events

By creating an event activity directly from the events box, on the home page the individual is able to feature the up and coming event in just one step.

Typing in the event intended into the "what are you planning" space on the right hand column of the home page, will allow all those visiting the page to be privy to the information and then they can decide if the event is a suitable platform for them to meet and arrange possible dates.

Hey There Socialite!

On the form that opens up, the individual can then type in further information about the event such as the time and place of the intended event and the general description of what it is all about.

This will then give all those interested in attending a general idea of what is going to take place and the possible types of crowd it is going to draw. This information is also important to the individual looking to make a connection for the purpose of dating.

There are generally two types of events popularly featured on the facebook platform, and these would include public events where the invitations are usually extended to anyone and everyone, and there are the private events where only invited people are privy to the information posted about the event.

Both these style are great ways to meet people and get dates but the individual must be alert to these events being feature in order to know where and when this dating possibility can be initiated.

CHAPTER 7- LOVE AND FOURSQUARE SOCIAL MEDIA

Any event organized needs the support of the people attending to ensure its success. Today it is possible to reach a wider circle of people for the intention of presenting invitations that will encourage them to attend these events. This can be done in a variety of ways that are more commonly less expensive than the more conventional methods, and one of these would be with the use of the foursquare platform.

Great Info

Foursquare is a service that users would find very useful and twitter followers are one of the areas where a buzz has been created for this style of sharing and alerting users to information posted.

Basically is a marketing opportunity, as foursquare would make it a seamless way to tweet check in and accomplishments. This of course would be an advantage for those who would be interested in making such connections with like minded and similar interests' individuals.

Foursquare is able to effectively and regularly adjust its channel syndication strategy from twitter to facebook to push these notifications to the forefront while constantly finding the balance to ensure the element of spam is not tagged to it.

It is also a great form of marketing anything and everything thus effectively providing the users with the opportunity to further their own agendas such as possible dating platforms.

When it comes to actually facilitation possible meets, the foursquare agenda is designed to inform its users of specific events when checking in at major venues.

There are also prompts that will help people keep in touch or even reconnect with others when a specific amount of time has lapsed as the software will be able to detect such things.

There has been noticeable activity as a lot of interested parties are now using the platform to check in and view the events being featured.

This activity is push factor that is further encouraging the foursquare to plan even more precise product plan ahead of time where the intersection of people, place and time becomes a big part of the feature.

About The Author

Margaret Sanders is born and raised in the high-pace lifestyle of New York, NY. Margaret is a natural writer and loves to go out with her friends. During her high school days, she was a cheerleader and was loved by all. Margaret has more than enough confidence. She can withstand any type of crowd without fear of facing them. Because of this, Margaret was loved and admired by all.

Margaret noticed though that there are just some students who were ordinary, plain and thus often left behind and picked-on. She feels sorry for them. She then created a small organization to gather these types of students to help them boost their self-confidence.